*For Polly Hill,
in honor of her love of sea, boats, and gulls.
—S. M.*

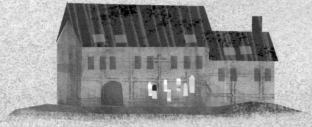

*For Zach and Ellie
and all ocean dreamers.
—A. S.*

SIMON & SCHUSTER BOOKS FOR YOUNG READERS
An imprint of Simon & Schuster Children's Publishing Division
1230 Avenue of the Americas, New York, New York 10020
Text © 2022 by Sy Montgomery
Illustration © 2022 by Amy Schimler-Safford
Book design by Chloë Foglia © 2022 by Simon & Schuster, Inc.
SIMON & SCHUSTER BOOKS FOR YOUNG READERS and related marks are trademarks of Simon & Schuster, Inc.
For information about special discounts for bulk purchases, please contact Simon & Schuster Special Sales at 1-866-506-1949 or business@simonandschuster.com.
The Simon & Schuster Speakers Bureau can bring authors to your live event. For more information or to book an event, contact the
Simon & Schuster Speakers Bureau at 1-866-248-3049 or visit our website at www.simonspeakers.com.
The text for this book was set in Wilke.
The illustrations for this book were rendered in watercolor, oil paints, oil pastels, collage and Photoshop.
Manufactured in China • 1221 SCP
First Edition
2 4 6 8 10 9 7 5 3 1
Library of Congress Cataloging-in-Publication Data
Names: Montgomery, Sy, author. | Schimler-Safford, Amy, illustrator.
Title: The seagull and the sea captain / Sy Montgomery ; illustrated by Amy Schimler-Safford.
Description: New York ; Simon & Schuster Books for Young Readers, [2022] | "A Paula Wiseman Book." | Audience: Ages 4-8 | Audience: Grades 2-3 |
Summary: "In a quiet harbor in New England, a sea captain named Ellis is   visited by a seagull. By the end of the week the seagull had retuned and was eating crackers
out of the captain's hand. They continued their friendship the entire season and the next year in the spring the gull retuned. After four years of friendship, the wild
seagull named Polly still visits. This unlikely story of a wild bird and a friendly sea captain reminds us how we are all connected"-- Provided by publisher.
Identifiers: LCCN 2021008139 (print) | LCCN 2021008140 (ebook) | ISBN 9781534482241 (hardcover) | ISBN 9781534482258 (ebook) Subjects:
LCSH: Polly Five Toes (Bird)—Juvenile literature. | Ellis, Heath—Juvenile literature. | Gulls—Massachusetts–Gloucester Harbor—Biography--Juvenile literature. |
Ship captains—Massachusetts—Gloucester Harbor—Biography—Juvenile literature. | Human-animal relationships—Massachusetts–Gloucester Harbor—
Juvenile literature. | Gloucester Harbor (Mass.)—Biography—Juvenile literature.
Classification: LCC QL696.C46 M67 2022 (print) | LCC QL696.C46 (ebook) | DDC 598.3/38097445--dc23
LC record available at https://lccn.loc.gov/2021008139
LC ebook record available at https://lccn.loc.gov/2021008140

The Seagull
and the Sea Captain

Sy Montgomery

Illustrated by
Amy Schimler-Safford

A Paula Wiseman Book

Simon & Schuster Books for Young Readers

New York   London   Toronto   Sydney   New Delhi

On a bright, blue-sky day, a sea captain steered his family's schooner out of Gloucester Harbor, riding the wind on the boat's four tall, white sails. What would he see that day? What wonders would he show his passengers? Everyone was on the lookout. There's so much to see: handsome mansions lining the harbor, motorboats and fishing boats and sailboats, colorful buoys bobbing on the waves.

Not far away, another group had set out on a voyage too. Gulls were riding the wind on their strong, outspread wings.

Gulls are always on the lookout too. There's so much to see: people eating yummy french fries on motorboats; fishermen hauling in nets, and pots of lobsters and crabs; shoals of little fish glittering just beneath the waves.

Onboard the schooner, passengers peered through binoculars and cameras. A grandfather was taking pictures of lighthouses. A little girl was watching out for whales.

Two friends were taking pictures of each other against the schooner's masts, sails, and lines.

From the sky, the gulls watched everything below. Three gulls chased an eagle, just for fun. Others dove for fish.

One gull was drawn to the four tall white sails of the schooner—as white as the satiny feathers on his own head, belly, and breast. The sails caught the wind just like his own strong, outspread wings.

The captain saw the gull fly close, then fold her wings into a V. The gull fanned his tail and stretched out his pink legs and webbed feet to land on one of the sails. Then the bird jumped down to the back of the boat, right next to the captain.

The gull looked at the captain. He was wearing a shirt as white as the sails of his ship. The gull thought the captain was a sharp dresser.

The captain looked at the gull. He admired the bird's sleek gray and white feathers. He thought the gull was a sharp dresser too.

But then the captain noticed something else. The gull was missing one toe on his right foot, an old injury that was now healed.

"Well, hello," said the captain to the seagull. "Are you hungry?"
The captain had some of his favorite snacks on board: oyster crackers. Maybe the bird would like them too! He tossed a cracker. The gull caught the treat in midair.

He looked the captain in the eye, as if to say "Thanks!" and then he flew away.

The next day, again the captain hoisted the big white sails of the schooner.
The next day, again the gulls left their night roosts, catching the wind in their wings.

From far away, the five-toed gull spotted
the four tall sails of the schooner. He
recognized the captain in his white shirt.
The gull thought, *My friend is back!*

The bird flew toward the schooner. *Plink!* He landed on the stern—right next to the captain at the wheel. The captain checked the bird's toes. On the left foot, three, like any gull. But on the right—just two. Five toes. The captain thought, *My friend is back!*

"Want a cracker?" the captain asked the gull. Indeed, he did—and the bird caught the cracker in midair.

The captain decided on a name for the gull. "Since you like crackers so much," said the captain to the gull, "I'll call you Polly. Polly Five Toes." The gull liked his new name. He liked the crackers, too. But most of all, he liked sailing on the beautiful white-winged schooner beside the captain— because everything is more fun with a friend.

Every day that summer, when the weather was fine, the schooner
set sail. And every day, Polly Five Toes came to visit the captain.
The passengers loved to see him. Sometimes Polly would just stay for
a minute. Sometimes he would stay for the entire two-hour journey,
enjoying the scenery with the captain and his guests.

No matter how long or short Polly would stay,
the captain looked forward to seeing him. He
loved sailing his schooner even more now—
because everything is more fun with a friend.

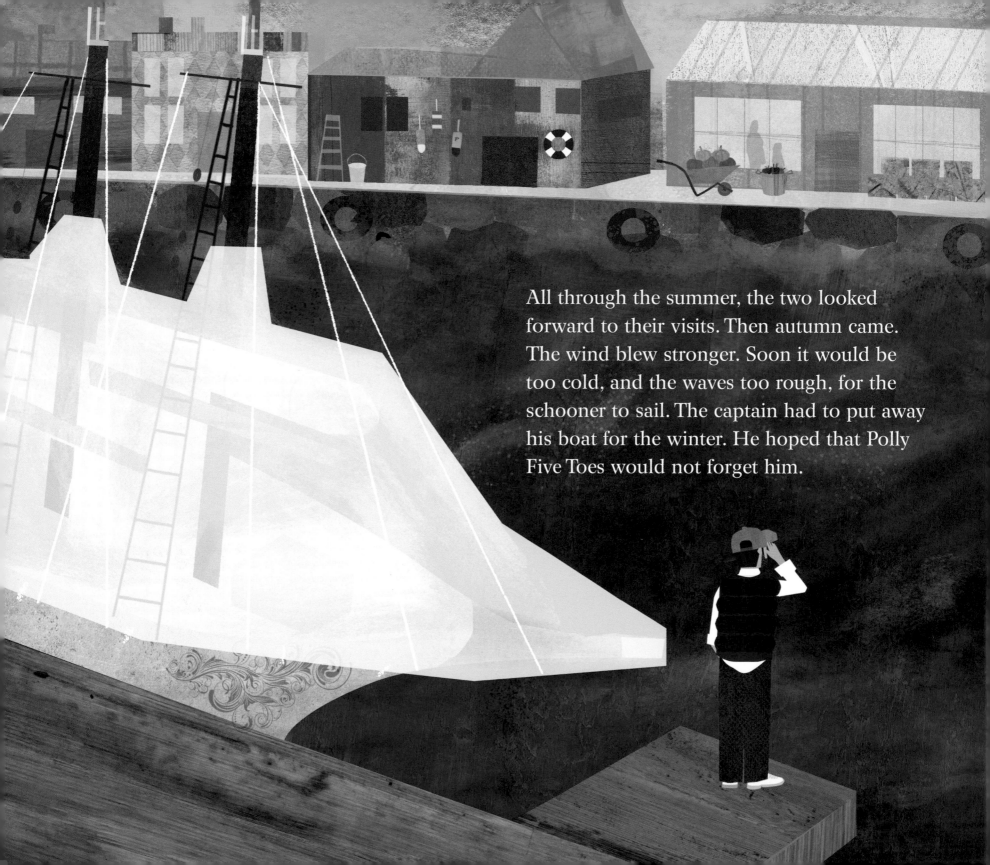

All through the summer, the two looked forward to their visits. Then autumn came. The wind blew stronger. Soon it would be too cold, and the waves too rough, for the schooner to sail. The captain had to put away his boat for the winter. He hoped that Polly Five Toes would not forget him.

As autumn came and the wind grew colder, Polly Five Toes, too, knew winter was coming. Soon it would be too cold to stay in Gloucester. Polly Five Toes had to fly south for the winter. He hoped that the captain would not forget him.

At last, the long New England winter ended, and the year turned to spring. The captain sailed his schooner, full of passengers celebrating Mother's Day. Passengers admired the handsome mansions lining the harbor, gazed at the motorboats and fishing boats and sailboats, and watched the colorful buoys bobbing on the waves.

But the captain was looking for
gulls, and one gull in particular.
One with just five toes.

The captain saw plenty of birds.
Black cormorants arrowing
across the water.

Black-headed, red-billed, laughing
gulls wheeling in the sky.

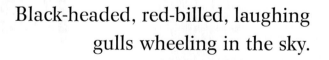

And there were plenty of herring gulls like Polly. But none approached the boat.

The next day, again the captain and his passengers set sail.
There was so much to see: mansions and boats and buoys, and
plenty of seabirds.

But no Polly.

Would the captain ever see his friend again?

On the third day he got his answer.

Polly Five Toes was back!

"Polly, want a cracker?" the captain asked. He already knew the answer. Polly Five Toes was glad for the snack. He had just flown a long way from his winter home farther south and was hungry. But he was even happier for the company of his friend. The two faced into the wind they loved, enjoying the ride even more than before—because everything's more fun with a friend.

And now every summer, from May to October, Polly Five Toes joins the captain on his schooner almost every day. Often he even sits on the captain's head! "That's the best view," explains the captain. Polly Five Toes enjoys the crackers, and also enjoys the view. But the best part, he agrees with the captain, is the journey together—because everything's more fun with a friend.

Polly Five Toes is a real herring gull and still regularly visits Captain Heath Ellis on the voyages he leads from Gloucester, Massachusetts, on his family schooner, the *Thomas E. Lannon*. They first met in 2013. You can learn more about Captain Ellis and the *Lannon* at www.schooner.org.

The Gen on Gulls:
• There are about fifty different kinds of gulls in the world, living on every continent, including Antarctica. The best-known of them all is the herring gull, with white breast, belly, and head, gray wings, yellow eyes, and pink legs and feet—the same kind as Polly Five Toes. Except most of them have six toes!

• Many people call all gulls "seagulls," but "seagull" is not really the name of a kind of gull at all. Not all gulls live near the sea. Some live thousands of miles from any seacoast.

• Gulls are smart, curious, and playful. They have learned to open the hard shells of clams by flying high over parking lots to drop them where the shells will break. Gulls like to investigate new things and often fly close to inspect objects of interest. They frequently chase other birds just for fun. And Polly Five Toes isn't the only gull to have befriended a person. There are other instances of gull-human friendships from around the world.

• Gulls eat lots of different foods (besides oyster crackers!). Their natural food includes fish, insects, clams, and crabs. But they also like french fries and pizza, though it isn't very good for them. One lady had a herring gull steal an entire lobster roll right out of her hand, and her photo of it happening became famous on the Internet!

• What to do if a gull wants to steal YOUR lunch? Look the bird right in the eye. Scientists did a study on this in Great Britain. They tested seventy-four herring gulls tempted with potato chips while a person paired with the bird either stared at the gull or looked away. Far more stole the chips when the person wasn't looking.

• Gulls can drink salt water. They prefer fresh, but can survive on seawater if that's all there is to drink. They spit the salt out their nostrils!

• Gulls live in large colonies with hundreds or thousands of individual gulls grouped together, like people in a city. Also like people, they choose one mate who they plan to stick with for life—though sometimes, also like people, they divorce. Divorces in gull colonies usually happen when a couple can't successfully raise babies together.

• Baby gulls hatch out of a simple nest on a beach, roof, or cliff. Polly Five Toes probably had one or two fluffy brother or sister chicks who hatched on a beach of sand and pebbles. The babies are closely (and noisily!) guarded by their parents. Males and females switch off incubating the eggs, protecting the chicks, and searching for food for their young.

• What is the red dot on Polly Five Toes's beak for? Adult herring gulls, and other kinds of gulls as well, develop this dot to help direct their chicks' attention to the parent's mouth to be fed. The parents don't have hands, so they bring food in their stomachs to their babies and then feed them beak-to-beak.

• In the winter, many herring gulls from a given colony migrate to warmer climes. But not all. Some stay just where they are.

• We don't know whether Polly Five Toes is male or female, because to our human eyes, the sexes look the same. But gulls know the difference at a glance. Birds can see colors we can't, including colors in the ultraviolet light spectrum, and to them, male herring gulls look much more colorful than females.

• Young gulls often look different from adult gulls for several years. Young herring gulls don't have Polly Five Toes's pure white head, belly, and chest. Instead, they are mottled brown.

• What happened to Polly Five Toes's missing toe? Nobody knows for sure, but it's likely that it got caught in discarded fishing line or plastic trash. When you clean up trash at the beach, you're protecting birds like Polly Five Toes—as well as fish, sharks, sea turtles, whales, and dolphins.

• With luck, Polly Five Toes will live a long time. There is even one record of a herring gull who lived twenty-nine years!